Devon Festivals

Robert Hesketh

Bossiney Books

First published 2017 by
Bossiney Books Ltd, 33 Queens Drive, Ilkley, LS29 9QW
ISBN 978-1-906474-58-4

Acknowledgements
All photographs are by the author, www.roberthesketh.co.uk
except that on page 9 which is by Simon Stuart.
The photo on the front cover is reproduced by courtesy of Matt Lemon, entertainer, from Braunton, that on the back cover by courtesy of Sophie Richardson, 'No.14', North Street, Ashburton.

Printed by R Booth Ltd, Penryn Cornwall

Wassailing in Sandford and Whimple

Wassailing apple trees to encourage pollination and a good crop is an ancient custom, a ritual of sympathetic magic. Traditionally held on Old Twelfth Night (January 17th), 'Wassail' derives from the Old English 'Wes Hal'. It means 'Be in good health' and is celebrated across England's apple counties, not least Devon.

'In the depths of winter, our ancestors worried whether they would ever see spring or blossoms again,' explained Barney Butterfield of Sandford Orchards. 'With wassailing, we salute the trees and ask for their bounty.'

Mark Bailey, Sandford Wassail's Green Man, appeared out of the night: 'The Green Man represents fertility and new life. I'm dressed in my Exeter Morris kit. Morris is all about fertility. Our clashing Morris sticks wake up the ground and our bells frighten away evil spirits.

'We begin with a torch lit procession through Sandford Square,' continued Mark. 'The King and Queen are crowned and we move on to wassail Town Barton Orchard, putting toast in the tree for the birds to pollinate it and nourishing the roots with cider. We sing the wassail song and make as much noise as possible.'

> Old apple tree, we wassail thee
> And hoping thou wilt bear…
> So merry let us be, let every man
> Take off his hat and shout
> To the old apple tree.

And shout they do, accompanied by draughts of cider, plus plenty of whooping and whistling, banging pots and sticks and firing guns.

'The Whimple Wassail song was the first thing that inspired me,' said folk musician Jim Causley, born in the village long famous for its cider orchards. 'It's traditional and very old. Like wassails themselves, West Country wassailing songs vary, but they have a similar theme and words, singing to the apple trees and asking for a good harvest.

'Our wassail has a good first line:

> Wassail, wassail, the moon she shines down…

'And the second verse goes:

> O old apple tree prosper, bud, bloom and bear
> That we may have plenty of cider next year

And where there's a barrel, we hope there'll be ten
So that we may have cider when we come again.'

Jim led the singing from Whimple's New Fountain Inn and the torch lit procession started its round of several orchards, each brightly lit with its own bonfire. Cider-soaked toast was put in the branches to attract birds to pollinate the trees; the Prince and Queen recited their verses and threw apples at the trees. Everyone raised a great shout and we banged our pots and pans with gusto. Just in case the evil spirits failed to get the message, we concluded with a deafening five gun volley that split the night in a flash of fire.

Tip Tip Toeing in Gittisham

'Tip tip toe, please for a penny and away we'll go!' cry Gittisham children as they call door to door around the village on Shrove Tuesdays. They share all the money they raise and some villagers give them sweets too.

'It's like trick or treating without the costumes,' explained Gittisham mum Carol Hall. 'Tip Tip Toeing is a living tradition. If it lapses, that will end it, so we must keep it going.'

No one knows why Tip Tip Toeing is called such, nor its origins, though oral history shows the custom dates to at least the 1880s. The fun starts with hot dogs and cakes in Gittisham Hall (provided by village mums) as soon as the children get back from school in Feniton and Honiton and continues into the evening as children call on houses around the village.

When Gittisham School was still open, children were given a half holiday. After church, they walked all around the parish, some five miles, as 82 year old Sid Philips recalled:

'During the war we had evacuees down from London. One year we went Tip Tip Toeing and found they'd beaten us to it, made their own collecting tin and pinched all the customers. It was all right in the end though: they were made to give all the money back!'

Gig racing in Dartmouth

Gigs are fast rowing boats designed to pilot sailing ships into harbour – though smugglers also found them ideal for landing cargoes and evading the Revenue. By custom, the first gig to reach a ship got the job. The competition this fostered blossomed into an organised sport after 1838 when Cornish boat builder W Peters created a new design he considered perfection. His gig was named *Treffry* and is still raced by Newquay Rowing Club. All gigs that compete today under Cornish Pilot Gig Association rules must conform to *Treffry* specifications: six oars, 32 ft long, and beam 4 ft 10 in. Gig racing is a popular and fast growing sport and the Association has clubs throughout the South West, including eleven in Devon.

Each club's gig racing course is different, but timed to last around 15 minutes. Some are on rivers, some on the open sea. At Dartmouth, teams start from the harbour and race down the Dart estuary to the castle and back, a course that demands considerable skill to negotiate the currents, bends and buoys. With many competing clubs and separate races for men's, women's and mixed teams, as well as veterans, juniors and other special classes, races continue all afternoon and provide much varied entertainment.

Dartmouth's main regatta is held in late August and includes river, fun, sports and children's events as well as music and fireworks.

Lustleigh May Day

Every year a new May Queen is crowned in Lustleigh and the ancient traditions of welcoming spring are renewed. Tradition is the watchword: each Queen is a Lustleigh girl and holds court beneath her canopy of flowers on the rock in Lustleigh Orchard, seated on a throne of Dartmoor granite.

Headed by Village Crier Dave Wills, a brass band leads the procession through Lustleigh, followed by the Queen and her entourage. Next come the children and last the public. The Rector blesses the May Queen – before blessing everyone else with liberal lashings of water.

Maypole dancing begins to music by a village band. Other entertainments include duck racing, hoop-la and Morris dancing. The village mummers perform a play showing the eternal battle between summer and winter and the children have a thumping good tea with home baked cakes.

Lustleigh's May Day is essentially the same as a century ago. It's the annual event that brings all the Lustleigh children together – something that's been missing since the village school closed a generation ago.

'May Day's very cohesive,' said Sara Pelling, whose daughter, Abby, (below) is a former Queen. 'It gives the village a great sense of community and is so much fun. Everyone gets involved, working hard to make the day a success. It seems old fashioned, but then it's a traditional event.'

This festival of the coming summer has a long and curious history. It began as 'Beltane', a full-blooded pagan rite, when flocks and herds were put out to summer pastures. During the Middle Ages, it reached an uneasy truce with the Church. However, Puritans regarded the maypole as 'a stinking idol'. In 1644 Parliament banned maypoles altogether. May festivities were restored with Charles II in 1660, but suffered a general decline in the 18th century. However, the Victorian vogue for 'Merrie England' encouraged a widespread revival under the combined patronage of squire, parson and schoolmaster.

A few May festivals, such as the 'Obby 'Oss (an obvious fertility symbol) in Padstow, Cornwall and Minehead in Somerset, retain some pagan flavour, but Lustleigh's May Day is a gentler affair. True, it keeps the pagan custom of 'bringing in the May', through placing summer flowers around the May Queen's canopy, as well as Morris dancing and village sports, but its central figure is young and maidenly.

History and symbolism aside, it is the pleasure of music, dancing and games in an idyllic setting that draws so many people to Lustleigh every May Day. 'It's all about having a delightful day out,' said local resident Belinda Baudouy. 'The atmosphere's very country and village.'

Wormcharming at Blackawton

Blackawton's International Wormcharming Festival is held each Sunday before the May Day Bank Holiday to raise funds for Devon Air Ambulance and other charities. The rules are simple: each team consists of three members, a Charmer, a Catcher and a Counter.

After five minutes 'worming up time', the teams have fifteen minutes to charm as many worms as they can from the one metre square plots. Contraptions and potions are permitted, also singing, dancing, skipping or almost any other activity to induce the wrigglers to show. The winners are those who catch the most worms. Two Judges and an official Worm Master enforce discipline, whilst an official Cheat, aided by a Junior Cheat, do their best to undermine such officiousness… and are rumoured to sell pre-dug worms for a suitable inducement.

After returning the worms to their rightful homes, competitors can repair to Worm HQ (the Normandy Arms) or to the George Inn's Music and Beer Festival for some worming down. Other attractions include the Fun Dog Show, face painting and a barbeque. Each year's Wormcharming has a different fancy dress theme and concludes with an auction of unlikely items for charity.

Hunting the Earl of Rone in Combe Martin

Hunting the Earl of Rone takes place over four days of Spring Bank Holiday. It is a unique custom, involving the Grenadiers, Hobby Horse, Fool and costumed dancers hunting the Earl through Combe Martin. Finally found on Monday night, he is mounted backwards on a donkey and paraded through the village. Often shot by the Grenadiers, he's revived by the Fool and Hobby Horse and re-set on the donkey. Fatally shot on the beach, the Earl is thrown into the sea.

There are several conflicting theories explaining the Earl's identity. Possibly, he was Hugh O'Neill, Earl of Tyrone, who was forced to flee Ireland in 1607. According to local legend, O'Neill was shipwrecked in nearby Raparee Cove and hid in the woods until captured by Grenadiers sent from Barnstaple.

Unfortunately, there is no historical evidence to back this theory. It has also been suggested the Hunt began as a Pagan, Green Man custom (see page 14), or is the remnant of medieval May Games (page 6). Another suggestion is that the Earl was a local landowner, a Chichester, who was Lord Deputy of Ireland in O'Neill's time. (See the Earl of Rone website for fuller discussion.)

Pixie Day at Ottery St Mary

Scores of Brownies and Cubs re-enact the Pixies' Revenge in Ottery St Mary on the Saturday closest to Midsummer. Legend has it that the growing power of the medieval Church led to increasing tension with East Devon's long established Pixie community, who preferred the old Pagan ways. The conflict intensified once Bishop John de Grandisson established the splendid church of St Mary in 1337.

Matters came to a head in 1454 when bells were ordered for the new church. Above all things, Pixies cannot abide the sound of church bells. They succeeded in capturing the monks bringing the bells to Ottery and led them towards the cliffs at Sidmouth, where the monks would have fallen to their destruction had not one monk stubbed his toe and cried 'God bless my soul!' This broke the Pixie spell; the monks turned inland to Ottery and the bells were hung in St Mary's tower.

Thwarted, the Pixies took revenge by creeping silently up to St Mary's, capturing the bell ringers and imprisoning them in a Pixie cave. By great good fortune and God's blessing, the ringers escaped.

Their successors have continued to ring the church bells, 'The poor man's only music [which] rang from morn to evening all the hot fair day' in Samuel Taylor Coleridge's poem 'Frost at Midnight', in part of which he fondly remembers Ottery, the town of his birth and early childhood.

Pixie Day begins early afternoon with a fair in the Land of Canaan. This includes stalls, live music, refreshments, children's games and a beer tent. Hordes of Pixies pour into the town square as evening draws on. After a noisy melée, they head for the church, capture the ringers and raise a full throated cry, the ear splitting qualities of which have to be heard to be fully understood.

Happily, the ringers escape and the Pixies are reduced to civilised behaviour with entertainment in the town square. When I visited, this was ably provided by Elphic the Jester, an accomplished juggler, both on and off his monocycle. Weather permitting, the day concludes with a grand firework display in the Land of Canaan. All funds raised during the day go to the Scout and Guide movements in the town.

Ale Tasting and Bread Weighing in Ashburton

Ashburton's annual Ale Tasting, Bread Weighing and Medieval Fair are fixed for the third Saturday in July. The procession is led by the City of Exeter Pipe Band. Ashburton's Portreeve with members of the Courts Leet and Baron Jury, each resplendent in medieval costume, walk with them, visiting the seven hostelries and five bakeries in town to check that the bread and ale are up to standard.

Uniformed marshals with long staves rap loudly on each inn door three times before the Master Bailiff orders the landlord or landlady (some lords appear as ladies) to produce two tankards of their best ale. These days, all are glad to comply, but one Joanna Cooke refused point blank in 1788.

Ale is both tasted and poured over a wooden bench for the Ale Tasters to sit in. If their leather breeches stick to the bench that's taken as a sign the ale is adulterated. When the Tasters judge the ale favourably, the inn is awarded a certificate along with a sprig of evergreen to hang over the entrance.

Today, all is in good humour, but an Ashburton brewer was fined for sticky ale in the thirteenth century. Evidently, Tasters had serious work to do in the days before factory inspectors and food hygiene regulations. For instance, the Portreeve's records for 1747 show Ashburton's ale tasters attended 335 brewings – unsurprising as the town had up to thirty inns and most brewed their own ale.

Ashburton's Master Bailiff demands loaves from each bakery; then the Bread Weighers assess them in massive iron balances. Finding the bread of good weight, they award the baker a certificate. By late afternoon, a great basket of bread has been gathered and is auctioned by a professional auctioneer, whose rapid patter is an entertainment in itself. Proceeds go to the Portreeve's chosen charity.

After the tasting and weighing comes the Medieval Fair with stalls selling refreshments and local produce. Other entertainments include juggling, live music and Morris dancing. Members of the Court Leet and ticket holders conclude the day with a medieval banquet.

Holsworthy too has an annual Ale Tasting in July where Tasters visit every inn and sample the beer. The following morning, the Town Crier opens St Peter's fair by reading out James I's market charter. Bread Weighing and the Pretty Maid competition are also part of the events. Ale is also tasted every year in **Hatherleigh**.

Pilton Green Man Day

Green Man Day is a friendly village event celebrating the charter granted to Pilton for a market and fair by Edward III in 1344. It begins with a procession led by the Green Man and the Town Crier, accompanied by costumed musicians, dancers and two men bearing huge masks, one red and one green. From Barnstaple Square the procession winds its way along High Street and Pilton Causeway into Pilton village – long ago overtaken in size by 'upstart' Barnstaple. It continues up Pilton Street, lined with many stalls selling food and drinks, and stops in the gardens of Pilton House, where the pageant is enacted.

Pilton's Green Man is resplendent in leaves and flowers and walks on stilts – no mean feat given the distance covered. Like the Green Man carving in St Mary's, Pilton, which inspired local people to develop Green Man Day in the 1980s and 90s, he represents seasonal change, the life force and Nature, according to Pilton resident Hamish Patrick. Thus, it's very appropriate to have Green Man day in July, when Nature is at her zenith.

'Everyone interprets the Green Man Day differently,' said Helen Clark-Hayton, who lives nearby. 'It's connected with seasonal change and the clash between Christianity and Paganism… this is what the pageant is about.'

The pageant in Pilton House grounds features an ensemble of performers in red, headed by the Pilton Prior, and an opposing ensemble in green led by the Green Man. The encounter is mimed rather than spoken to suggest questions in the stand-off between the old religion and the new, between Pagan and Christian – questions such as 'Did the old religion really die?' – questions which are also implied at Lustleigh's May Day (page 6) and at Pixie Day in Ottery St Mary (page 10).

As the pageant unfolds, conflict gives way to a resolution between the Green Man and the Church. The Green Man carving on the chancel screen at Pilton and many other churches up and down the country also implies an accommodation was reached, that elements of the old ways were absorbed in the new religion.

Calendar of Events

January

Wassailing the apple trees at Whimple and Sandford (page 2)

February

Tip Tip Toeing, Gittisham (page 4)

April

Dartmouth Gig Regatta (page 5)

May

Lustleigh May Day (page 6)
Wormcharming, Blackawton (page 8)
Hunting the Earl of Rone, Combe Martin (page 9)
Devon County Show

June

Pixie Day, Ottery St Mary (page 10)

July

Ale Tasting and Bread Weighing, Ashburton and Holsworthy (page 12)
Green Man Day, Pilton (Barnstaple) (page 14)
Apple Pie Day, Marldon (page 18)
Hot Pennies Day, Honiton (page 19)
Sidmouth Folk Week (lasts into August) (page 20)

August

Dartmoor Folk Festival, South Zeal (page 20)
Dartmouth Royal Regatta

September

Widecombe Fair (page 22)

October

Baring Gould Folk Festival, Okehampton (page 24)
Apple Day, Hennock (page 26)
Tavistock Goose Fair (page 27)
Bampton Charter Fair (page 30)

November

Hatherleigh Carnival, including Blazing Tar Barrels (page 28)
Ottery St Mary Carnival, including Blazing Tar Barrels (page 28)
Turning the Devil's Stone, Shebbear (page 31)
Finch Foundry St Clement's Day, Sticklepath (page 32)

The events covered

Devon has a huge number of festivals and other events, ranging from ancient pagan survivals to modern literary and music festivals. In this book we have concentrated on those which are oldest and most traditional in character.

Useful Websites

Visit Devon
Information Britain

Marldon Apple Pie Fair

Apple Pie Fair originated in the late 19th century. During the apple season, trader George Hill rode his donkey from Marldon to the weekly market at St Marychurch, his panniers full of apples. For the Marychurch Fair, he arrived with a cart containing a huge oval apple pie (reputedly the size of a kitchen table) drawn by two donkeys wearing harness and reins decorated with plaited straw.

Not to be outdone, Marldon's annual Show featured a huge apple pie from 1888. After a lapse, Apple Pie Fair was revived in 1958 to raise funds for the village hall. Following tradition, the Fair begins from the parish church with a procession including the magnificent Pie drawn on a cart, Apple Jacks (scarecrows who protect the apple trees), musicians and three Princesses. The procession winds its way through the various stalls on Jubilee Meadow, the Princesses are crowned and the pie is cut.

In addition to apple pie, there is a wide range of food and drink on sale through the day, plus animal and bird displays and stalls selling bric-a-brac and books. Other entertainments include a dog show, dancing, the Apple Olympics and a sheepdog display.

Honiton Hot Pennies

'Oyez, oyez! The glove is up! The fair has begun! No man shall be arrested until the glove is taken down! God save the Queen!'

Thus yells Honiton's Town Crier, Dave Retter, as he raises the flower decorated glove of plenty (symbolising a good harvest) and offers the traditional amnesty to debtors to encourage people to come to town and buy from the market stalls. Hot pennies are then thrown from the windows of Honiton's inns, to be eagerly collected in the crowded High Street.

No one knows the origins of the hot pennies (luke-warm these days for safety reasons), but it is thought that medieval gentry threw hot chestnuts or small coins to hungry serfs for amusement. Traditionally, the hot pennies opened Honiton's Agricultural Fair. However, livestock have not been sold in High Street for many years, though Dave would like to see this revived – but not the wife sale recorded in 1828, when Mrs Broom went for £1.

Held in late July, Hot Pennies Day is preceded by Market Charter Day. This celebrates the 1247 charter and has stalls, music, a classic car rally, dog show and town crier competition.

Sidmouth Folk Week

'Sidmouth Folk Week is a diverse festival of music and dance from around the British Isles, featuring grass roots elements through to internationally renowned performers,' said Press Officer Sarah Coxson at the start of what proved to be a very entertaining and lively visit to one of Britain's longest established (1954) and most popular folk festivals. Visitors have a huge range of choice through the week, from traditional folk music to cutting edge performances. There are also acts from countries as diverse as America, Italy, Belgium and Latvia.

'I probably wouldn't be a folk musician without the inspiration of Sidmouth from childhood onwards,' said Jim Causley, whom I'd met earlier in the year at the Whimple Wassail (page 2). 'I'm proud we have England's most famous folk festival here in Devon, where I grew up. I particularly like the traditional English dance bands. The atmosphere's great, not least among the impromptu acts in the streets and on the Esplanade.'

As well as major concerts, there are small intimate sessions, many held in local pubs. There are also ceilidhs, Morris and other folk dancing, roots parties, storytelling and family entertainments including acrobats and – for the first time in 2016 – a hobby horse parade.

Sidmouth's handsome sea front is lined with stalls selling a wide variety of food, plus arts and crafts with a folky flavour. There is ample opportunity to wander at leisure, meeting musicians and dancers, imbibing the atmosphere of folk culture and learning more about it through hands-on workshops in making music and dancing. A large range of musical instruments is on display in the marquees and can be tried as well as bought. Many performers sell recordings of their music.

Scheduled for the start of the school summer holidays, Sidmouth Folk Week succeeds in being a family event with an extensive children's programme. This includes crafts such as puppet making and classes in singing, broom dancing, sword dancing, Cajun, playing the spoons, yoga and much besides.

Some artists go from Sidmouth to the **Dartmoor Folk Festival at South Zeal**, which follows on directly and lasts from Friday evening through Saturday and Sunday. Devon performers, local music, songs and dances are prominent at the Dartmoor Festival, founded by Dartmoor musician Bob Cann in 1977 to preserve and promote local musical traditions. The festival has grown and thrived, but remains a very warm and local event.

Widecombe Fair

Scheduled for the second Tuesday in September, Widecombe Fair lives up to its billing as a 'celebration of traditional Dartmoor life' with a very full programme lasting all day and late into the evening. The earliest *written* record of the fair discovered so far dates to 1850.

Undoubtedly, the well-known comic folk song 'Widdicombe Fair' in which Uncle Tom Cobley and his friends borrow Tom Pearce's old grey mare and ride her to Widecombe, helped spread the fair's fame far beyond Dartmoor and to make it one of Devon's largest festivals. First published about 1880, 'Widdicombe Fair' was collected by Rev. Sabine Baring Gould (page 24). Since 1929, Uncle Tom Cobley – who was a well-known farmer and huntsman from Spreyton, where he was buried in 1844 – has appeared in costume at the fair riding his white mare.

Farming and country life are the themes of Widecombe Fair. Animals are judged to find the best of their classes, with local breeds such as Dartmoor Whiteface sheep, South Devon cattle and Dartmoor ponies to the fore. There are sheepdog displays, a parade of hounds, gun dog and dog agility competitions and much more besides, including a hawking display and a spectacular show from the Dartmoor Hill Pony Display Team.

Demonstrations of traditional rural skills such as thatching and hay rick building are another attraction. There are parades of vintage tractors, cars and motorbikes. Country games are represented by terrier and ferret racing, bale tossing and tug o' war. The Uncle Tom Cobley Novelty Race is a unique cross-country event run from the top of Widecombe Hill to the Fair Field via rocks, gorse and bracken.

Meanwhile, there is Morris dancing and a day long programme of country music, featuring several musicians, several of whom also appear at Sidmouth and Dartmoor folk festivals (page 20) and the Baring Gould Folk Festival (page 24).

There is a huge variety of stalls. Again, country life is the theme with country clothing, cider, local produce, local books and crafts such as hand carved walking sticks. Devon charities and organisations such as Devon Air Ambulance and Widecombe Local History Group are well represented too and there are always refreshments on hand: teas, cakes, coffee and local ales in the beer tent, pasties, a hog roast and more.

A member of the Dartmoor Hill Pony Display Team

A keen competitor in the dog agility contest

The vintage car display

Okehampton: the Baring Gould Folk Festival

Held in late October, the festival spans a weekend and several venues in Okehampton, including halls, churches and pubs. As well as concerts and dances, there are singing and instrumental sessions, youth events, Morris dancing and a conker competition, plus the festival feast followed by a grand ceilidh.

It is a chance to participate as well as to be entertained, to practise singing, dancing and instrumental skills with the help of experienced folk musicians and dancers from the West Country and beyond. All ages and levels of experience are welcomed in the varied workshops, which may range from choir rehearsal to folk electronica and Latvian dancing.

A week long Folk Song School follows the festival, which is organised by Okehampton-based folk arts charity Wren Music, who named it in honour of Sabine Baring Gould, Rector and Squire of Lewtrenchard in West Devon from 1881 to 1924.

Baring Gould employed his considerable talents and deep interest in all things Devonian through his work in music, folklore, fiction, drama, history, archaeology, architecture and church restoration.

'The recovery of our West Country melodies has been the principal achievement of my life,' he wrote, recalling his long journeys in all weathers, collecting songs from country people in Devon and Cornwall. By far the best known (and least altered) is *Widdicombe Fair* – indeed, the adventures of Uncle Tom Cobley and all have become inseparable from Devon's identity (see page 22).

'Songs collected by Baring Gould are a silver thread running through the festival,' said Paul Wilson, Music Director of Wren. 'Among his best known are *Barbara Allen*, *Lord Bateman*, *The Raggle Taggle Gipsies*, *Ragged Beggarman*, *The Bells of North Lew*, *Fathom the Bowl* and my favourite, *Captain Ward*. He was the first to give Devon a decent profile in the history of folk song.'

'We owe him a great debt,' agreed Lester Simpson, a regular guest musician at the festival. 'Without him and other first generation collectors, many folk songs and tunes would have been lost forever.'

'Folk music is a live tradition,' explained Paul, 'an expression of ordinary people's trials, tribulations, aspirations and hopes. They are still pertinent to our society… they help us to cope, which is why I'm particularly keen to promote live performance.'

Hennock's Apple Day

As well as holding its annual Fayre, Hennock celebrates apples every October, freshly picked in local orchards. The Grand Hennock Bake Off is an apple pudding and pie competition open to all and there's a painting competition for the children: subject, apples. Many varieties of apple are on sale, as well as garden vegetables, local honeys, sausages and bacon. The barbeque provides pork and apple burgers, the tea stall apple cakes and cream, the bar cider and juice pressed at the previous year's Apple Day.

Roger Hooper and Sue White bring sacks of their traditional Devon cider apples such as Tremlett's Bitter, Pig's Snout, Slap Me Girdle and Harry Masters on a trailer. Their old fashioned screw press and petrol driven crusher were picked up cheaply in farm sales – a reflection that the days when cider orchards, presses and barns were usual on Devon farms, and farm labourers commonly enjoyed two quarts of cider per day as part of their wages, are now passed. Using wooden forms and specially made hessian sacks, Roger, Sue and their willing band of helpers build a cheese of crushed apples. Golden juice froths and gurgles into the tank below. It's delicious, both sharp and sweet – hardly surprising as natural sugars in the apples will produce cider with 6 1/2 % to 7 1/2 % alcohol.

Tavistock's Goose Fair

Tavistock's annual Goose Fair dates back as far as 1105, when Henry I authorised the monks of Tavistock Abbey to hold a weekly market. In 1152, Henry II granted Tavistock a three day market on St Rumon's feast in August. Later, this was moved to Michaelmas (September 29) and thence to the second Wednesday in October with the change to the Gregorian calendar in 1752.

As well as giving farmers a chance to sell livestock including geese to fatten for Christmas, Goose Fair was and is a major social event, drawing traders and visitors from a wide area. A park and ride scheme operates. Tavistock's main streets are closed to traffic and filled with stalls selling all manner of goods, such as clothes, toys, plants, crafts and bric-a-brac, as well as local produce, street food and drinks. Other attractions include live music, palmists, fortune tellers and a hog roast. Traditional fairground amusements such as dodgems, a Ferris wheel, shooting galleries and fairground rides keep going late into the evening.

Animals, including Dartmoor ponies, are shown at the Livestock Centre, and geese are auctioned along with many varieties of poultry. To avoid congestion, the sheep and cattle auctions are now held on different days close to Goose Fair.

Hatherleigh Carnival

Famous for its blazing tar barrels and its beautifully made and highly imaginative carnival floats, processed by torchlight through the town, Hatherleigh Carnival is a day-long event that draws visitors from a wide radius. Now held on the second Saturday in November, the Carnival combines fundraising for local charities with Guy Fawkes Night.

Preparations begin on Friday evening when the fuel-soaked barrels are processed through the town, led by Hatherleigh Silver Band in bizarre costume. The first barrels are set alight before dawn on Saturday and dragged on sleds through the streets at speed. Later in the morning, Eggesford Hunt meets in the square. Next, town criers from all over Devon gather in full regalia for a contest of skill and wit. After lunch, the children's procession moves through town to the packed Community Centre, where the Carnival Royalty are crowned. The children's floats and walking guys are judged: standards are very high.

Night falls and Hatherleigh Silver Band assembles with other bands. The main format has not changed greatly since Hatherleigh Carnival was started in 1903. The next year, the *Exeter Flying Post* reported how 'the procession was of unusual length and interest, including several new and novel items, special prizes were offered for the best "get up" and competition was keen'. It describes how the procession 'contained guys carrying torches, banners etc. headed by the town brass band, the carriages, bicycles, perambulators etc. mingling with the torch bearers.'

The procession moves to Hatherleigh's huge market, where visitors admire the floats, refresh themselves and enjoy the fun fair. Anticipation builds for the second run of blazing tar barrels. Fast and furious, this speeds through the crowd-lined street to the market, where the day ends in the flames and sparks of a massive bonfire.

The West Country has a history of torchlight processions and burning barrels. Associated with the defeat of the Gunpowder Plot in 1605, these fiery festivities may have far older, possibly Pagan roots.

Ottery St Mary's Carnival and Blazing Tar Barrels parallel Hatherleigh's, with two important differences. In Ottery, the Carnival with its torchlight procession is held on the Saturday before November 5th, whilst the Blazing Tar Barrels begins at dawn when cannon are fired and the barrels are carried on the rollers' shoulders as they dash through the crowded streets – an even more visceral experience than Hatherleigh's flame filled night!

Bampton Charter Fair

Bampton had two annual fairs until the 19th century. Held on the last Thursday in October, the present fair was already old when it gained a Royal Charter in 1258. Bampton Charter Fair was opened by Proclamation (a custom revived in 2004) and held under the jurisdiction of the Lord of the Manor and his steward. They collected fair tolls – which are still due to the Lord, though today they are distributed to voluntary organisations in the parish.

The Lord's court, known as Pieds Poudreux ('Dusty Feet') as justice was administered before the dust was off one's feet, is no longer part of the Charter Fair. Once the largest sheep fair in the West Country and famous too for cattle, Bampton Fair evolved into Bampton Pony Fair from the 1880s to the 1980s.

It continues to thrive today, but is focussed on crafts, local produce and entertainments. Crafts are sold and demonstrated in the church and in the streets, which are closed to traffic and full of stalls selling local produce, clothes, bric-a-brac and more besides. Entertainments include Punch and Judy, a magician, street art and a fun fair. There is folk music too, which continues in a folk festival on three following days.

Turning the Devil's Stone in Shebbear

Shebbear has its own unique celebration on Guy Fawkes Night, when the one tonne Devil's Stone is ritually turned by a team of bellringers armed with crowbars, thus celebrating the triumph of good over evil. First, Shebbear's church bells are rung discordantly.

The villagers gather at the Devil's Stone Inn and walk to the village green, where the Vicar retells how the mighty angel Lucifer (aka the Devil) grew too proud and vied with God. Lucifer and his legions fought against the heavenly host. Defeated, he descended to Shebbear, where he was struck by the Devil's Stone, hurled from Heaven by the Archangel Michael.

According to legend the Devil's Stone – a glacial erratic unlike any other rock in the area – traps the Evil One safely, but only for a year. Thwarted, but not wholly defeated, the Devil spends the next twelve months digging down and up to the other side of the Stone – at which point it must be turned to crush him again or ill fortune will plague the village.

Finch Foundry, Sticklepath, and St Clement's Day

Blacksmiths from the West Country and beyond gather at Finch Foundry to demonstrate their craft on St Clement's Day in late November. Clement was martyred by being thrown into the sea with an anchor roped to his neck. To expiate guilt at having forged the fatal anchor, he was adopted as the blacksmiths' patron saint.

Working hammer and tongs, the smiths turn red hot metal into a remarkable array of handsome objects, from pokers and candlesticks to doorknockers, firedogs, hooks and even flowers, proving the blacksmith's ancient skills are very much a living tradition.

'Firing the Anvil' is part of that tradition and celebrated every hour with a bang when a small charge of black powder is detonated in the anvil to test its strength.

Finch Foundry, an early 19th century forge, provides an ideal venue for these celebrations. Open through the National Trust, it has been restored to full working order. All the machinery, including fan, shears, hammers and grinding wheel, is water-powered via wheels driven by water drawn through a leat from the River Taw.

Finch Foundry's museum of hand crafted tools, including scythes, billhooks and shovels, further testify to the smith's craft.